CHOSEN FOR A PURPOSE

Diretha Jennings

Printed in the United States of America
First Printing: November 2024
The Scribe Tribe Publishing Group

ISBN-978-1-958436-36-3 (print)
978-1-958436-37-0 (ebook)

CONTENTS

POWER

Introduction

Welcome, dear reader, to a journey of discovery, empowerment, and spiritual awakening. This book is more than just a collection of words; it is an invitation to embark on a transformative path, one that leads to understanding your true purpose, unlocking your immense potential, and harnessing the power within you.

In these pages lies a devotional designed to encourage, inspire, and inform. It's a guide tailored for anyone who might feel weighed down by life's trials and tribulations. Whether you're facing a mountain of challenges or navigating the complexities of everyday life, this book seeks to be your companion, offering solace and strength through God's word.

This devotional is structured around three fundamental pillars: Purpose, Potential, and Power. Each section delves into these themes, offering insights and reflections designed to ignite an inner fire within you. It's a call to not only discover who God created you to be but to pursue that vision with all your heart, leaving nothing on the table.

As you turn these pages, may you find not just words, but a source of strength and inspiration. Let this book be a daily reminder that your current state, no matter how daunting, does not define your destiny. Instead, through meditation and study of God's word, you can awaken to the incredible possibilities that lie within you.

Purpose

the reason for which something is created, or for which something exists

"For we are God's handiwork, created in Christ Jesus to do good works, which God prepared in advance for us to do. Ephesians 2:10 NIV

I Am Here On Purpose

In *Jeremiah 1:5*, God said to Jeremiah, *"Before I shaped you in the womb, I knew all about you. Before you saw the light of day, I had holy plans for you: A prophet to the nations—that's what I had in mind for you."* God informs Jeremiah that before he was even born, God knew him and had a purpose for him. The reason he was alive was determined before he entered the earth. The same is true for all of us. No one who has ever been born, was born by mistake. Whether your existence was planned by your parents, or you came as a surprise, you were meant to be here. Research shows that there is a 5% chance of conception when having unprotected sex. Since you were born and are alive, you are a part of the 5%. With such a low probability of conception, it's pretty safe to say that God really wanted you to be here. Your very existence was no mistake; according to Jeremiah 1:5, your purpose was created first, then you were created to ensure the purpose was carried out.

As you go through this devotional, keep in mind that you are here because God wanted you here. It does not matter how you got here, you are here. Not only are you here, but you are here on assignment. So now let's discover your purpose and live it out!

Prayer:
Lord, I thank you for choosing me. I know that because I was born and because I am here today, I have a purpose. Today and for the

rest of my life, I will live on purpose, your purpose. Use me Lord, I am a willing vessel. In Jesus' Name, Amen!

Affirmation:

I am chosen by God and I am here for His purpose.

Reflective Question:

What should I do to start living my life on Purpose?

Let It Work

"And we know that all things work together for good to those who love God, to those who are called according to his purpose."
Romans 8:28 KJV

We discovered that we are here on purpose. We now know that our purpose was created by God, then we were created by God to fulfill His purpose. We also know that life can be hard. We are faced with challenges daily and some of those challenges can be unbearable, sometimes life-changing. The scripture reminds us that if you love God and are called according to His purpose, the issues we face are beneficial to us.

Romans tells us that "all things" work together. Whatever experiences you have faced in life, good or bad, they are at work. From finding your true love to the loss of a loved one. Securing your dream job to losing everything you have worked so hard for. All things, everything is at work. The job of everything that happens in your life is to benefit you. It all works for your good.

This scripture is reassurance for those who love the Lord and have a purpose. Everything that happens to us is for our good. It all works together for our benefit. So when hard times come, don't get discouraged; it is God at work. He is using the good and the bad as tools of preparation for you. Moses had a hard life, his mother gave him away, he had a speech impairment, he even got into a heated situation and ended up killing a person. This act caused him to flee. All of these difficult experiences led him right to God, where he discovered his purpose. Had he not gone through those things, he would not have become the person God predestined to deliver the children of Israel.

What experiences have you had? No matter how hard they may have been, God lets us know in Romans 8:28, that it all is there for your benefit. So as a person who loves the Lord and has a God-given purpose, start looking at your situation, sit back and let them work, because its job is to benefit you.

Prayer:

God, thank you for every situation in my life, whether good or bad, past, present or future. I know that it all is for my benefit as a person who loves you and as a person who is living on purpose. Thank you for it all. In Jesus' Name, Amen!

Affirmation:

I am grateful for everything in my life because it is all there to benefit me.

Reflective Question:

What experiences have I had or am currently in the midst of that can be used for the purpose of good in my life?

Pressures And Problems

The pressures and problems we face within the parameters of our individual lives are part of the process. As believers we have allowed too many challenges we face to be debilitating, hindering our progression and maturity in the Lord. Pressure when applied properly can stop a person from bleeding out, can bind two items together, and can create a masterpiece.

- **Creative Pressure:** A pressure cooker is a great example of creative pressure. The concept of a pressure cooker is that a sealed pot accumulates steam inside to the put that it builds to a high pressure. The pressure inside then cooks the food in a shortened time. You can add your meats, vegetables, and starches with some seasoning, allow the pressure to build, and out comes a tasty meal. This same concept can be applied to your life. The things that have happened to you over time whether good or bad are part of your life and may have added welcomed or unwanted pressure, but when you add God to the mix, He uses it ALL to work out for your good. He uses the pressure to produce something beautiful and great because He loves you and has a purpose for your life. *And we know that all things work together for good to them that love God, to them who are the called according to [his] purpose. Romans 8:28 KJV*

- **Bonding Pressure:** Have you ever found yourself crying out for God even more when your back is against a wall? Or how about when you bond with someone over similar life struggles. There is a need to not face "this thing" alone and a desire for help along the way. Perhaps if that problem hadn't arisen and/or you didn't feel the pressure arising you may not have connected with God, family, or friends on a deeper level. Bonds that are created with a common goal of easing the pressures of life are necessary because we were not created to go through this life alone.

- **Life-Saving Pressures:** When a person is bleeding, whether it is a superficial cut or a deep wound, pressure is applied to stop the bleeding. The deeper the wound, the harder the pressure needs to be in order to prevent a person from bleeding out. Also, the length of time the pressure is applied is determined by the depth of the wound as well. There are pressures in life that unbeknownst to us have saved our lives. Have you ever felt so strongly that you needed to go a different route to work than normally? That was God preventing you from being in the midst of danger. Or perhaps you felt pressure in your chest and went to the emergency room and found out you were having some type of medical condition. Had there not been that pressure you may have died at home alone or traveled your usual route and encountered some danger that could have ended your life.

Prayer:
God, thank you for the different types of pressures I face in life. I now know that they all are there for my benefit. Help me to see things differently when I go through pressure situations. I am on a journey to my purpose and the pressures of life are all to my benefit. In Jesus' Name. Amen.

Affirmation:
I am grateful for the pressures of life because they all benefit me.

Reflective Question:
What is my immediate reaction when I am faced with the pressures of life? How can I respond differently?

Understanding The Purpose

When we understand our purpose and what God has ordained us to be, life can be so much better and more rewarding. Understanding is everything, and not from our perspective, but God's.

Trust in the LORD with all thine heart, and lean not unto thine own understanding. In all thy ways acknowledge him, and he shall direct thy paths. Proverbs 3:5-6 KJV

You see our understanding can be obscured by our own limited vision or lack thereof. So we must lean into understanding God's point of view about our lives and what He has created us to become. In order to understand God's point of view, we need to be studying and meditating on the word of God. In His word, we will find instructions, encouragement, and examples of how to live on purpose.

Even our intelligence can get in the way of our understanding causing us to try to understand God's way from a logical point of view as opposed to a faith perspective. Being logical may work when dealing with some ordinary day-to-day things, such as being on time for work, brushing your teeth, showering, not crossing the street when cars are coming, etc. There will be times when God will have you move in such a way that it seems to completely defy all logical reasoning. It is in these moments where many of us can miss the move of God in our lives that we have been praying for if we solely rely on our intelligence to help us to understand what God wants for us.

How does one step outside the comfort zone of intellectual reasoning?

1. **You must trust God completely, with child-like faith**, so that when God tells you what He wants from you, you will know that it *is* for your good.

2. **You have to spend time with God daily.** How can one begin to understand, know and form a bond with anyone if they have yet to spend time with them? The same is true of spending time with God; how can you know when God is speaking if you have not spent time in His presence to hear Him speak?

3. **You should read and meditate on the word of God every day.** You have to be able to align everything you hear with the word of God. Cross-referencing your ideas and thoughts with the word of God will help you to be aligned with **HIS** purpose for your life.

4. **You need to PRAY every day and even throughout the day.** (Think of prayers as talking with your best friend, your father, and your wise counsel all rolled into one.) Prayer is not just for when you need something from God. It is a daily conversation, a time of intimacy and vulnerability that will allow for your heart and mind to be one with God. Prayer is two-way communication. As you speak to God, you just allow Him to speak back to you.

Prayer:

God, help me to understand that you are in control. I trust you with my whole heart. I will not cloud my vision with my own perception of things, but I will rely on how You view things. You are in control of everything and because of that, all things will work for my benefit as I live out your purpose for me. Help me to trust you no matter how hard things may seem. In Jesus' Name. Amen.

Affirmation:

I choose to take God's perspective on everything.

Reflective Question:

Where in my life has my own way of thinking limited me from living in my purpose?

Forgive So You Can Move Forward

Forgiveness is a key part of your purpose. Forgiveness is not just about the other person, but about you and your personal purpose. When you have not forgiven, you will most likely harbor resentment and bitterness. These two combined can cause a hardened heart and lead to deception of who you are. Unforgiveness pours into every aspect of your life contaminating everything it touches. Unforgiveness can lead to mental, emotional, and physical sickness and disease as well "Dis-Ease."

> Scripture reminds us in **Proverbs 23:7: *For as he thinketh in his heart, so [is] he: Eat and drink, saith he to thee; but his heart [is] not with thee. KJV***

There is a misconception about unforgiveness that most experience and don't realize. It's the sense of feeling vindicated or even justified by holding onto your anger for what has been done to you. But there is no justice in holding on to the same knife you've been stabbed with and holding on to it from the cutting end, at that. That is what unforgiveness is doing to you in a spiritual and emotional sense. You are hurting yourself over and over again, all because you don't want to let go and forgive what has been done to you.

Prayer:

Father God, help me to forgive those who have trespassed against me as I have been forgiven of my sins. I pray both for my enemies and friends alike, that they may receive your grace by faith and be made whole. In Jesus' Name, Amen.

Affirmation:

I am forgiving because I have been forgiven.

Reflective Question:

Is there anyone that I am still holding a grudge against?

Persevere In Your Purpose

When we endure pain, we must remember the power of perseverance. Perseverance is to have tenacity. Therefore, you must be dedicated to persevering for your God-given Purpose. Understand why you were created. What is your purpose? What have you been called to do? So in this process, seek God's face to have a better understanding of his will and way of your life.

No one wants to experience pain on any level. Imagine being told that the pain you are feeling is for your good and has a purpose. Sounds ridiculous when you say it aloud. Yet, pain does have a purpose in our lives. Whether it's physical or emotional or mental, pain is usually an indicator that something is going on that needs further scrutiny. When your tooth aches, you are put on notice that you may have something serious going on with your teeth. You then call your dentist so that they can take a professional look at your mouth to determine what is going on. When you find yourself feeling sad all the time (for no apparent reason), this may make you aware that you may not be mentally or emotionally well and will require you to seek out a mental healthcare provider.

What if "life" itself is the source of your pain? Who do you seek then? How do you determine what level of pain you can handle? We honestly won't know how much pain we can handle until we are faced with certain situations that are painful and uncomfortable.

Being uncomfortable is where we will find our most significant growth if we allow our Heavenly Father to do just that–grow us in that pain.

1. Pain brings about Purpose
2. Pain produces growth
3. Pain makes us uncomfortable
4. Pain will draw us closer to the Lord

And we know that God causes everything to work together for the good of those who love God and are called according to his purpose for them. Romans 8:28 NLT

In order for us to see "the good" work together, we must persevere in our suffering. That is not easy to do by far because suffering will be painful and no one wants to endure pain longer than necessary. Yet, we do endure pain and for some of us, it's quite frequent, especially mothers. When you are giving birth to a child, that is the most painful experience. The contractions will make you feel close to death and pushing a tiny human out of your body is no small feat. Women around the world are giving birth daily, some without any pain medicine, and many of these women will have more children after their first one.

The pain of giving birth does not stop those mothers from pushing that precious baby out, nor does it stop most of them from having more children to build their families. This also applies to the pain/suffering we experience in life. We should not allow what we go through to stop us from pushing our way into purpose. When we persevere in our pain, we also get to see ourselves thrive in our purpose.

"Endurance is the power to see your way through a difficult and unfavorable set of circumstances."

What if I tell you we all have endurance and for some of us it may appear more evident than others because of situations where we had no choice but to press our way through? When you are in a life or death situation and you have to press your way until the end, you cannot just give up or you just might die. Whether we want to believe it or not, we are all in a life-or-death situation. If we do not choose to endure in this life we have been given, then we are making a choice to die. It may not be physical death, but you may just be in a state of existence. To exist is to be alive with no motivation, no drive, no determination. You're going through the motions.

To be driven by purpose is to be fueled by endurance that will see you through every obstacle and uncompromising situation. Think of it this way: You are driving the luxury vehicle called Purpose which is taking you on the journey of life. There will be many winding roads and obstacles that will occur because you cannot have a journey without some sort of adventure. In order to keep going on this journey, you must fuel your vehicle (purpose) with quality fuel or you won't go very far. That fuel is high-octane endurance which will help you to power through no matter what you face on your journey.

Prayer:

Father God, because I have a purpose, I know that the obstacles I faced and the uncompromising situations I've been placed in are stepping stones to lead to the milestones in my life. I realized that if you, God, do not change the situation, you will give me the strength to endure. And endure I shall! In Jesus' Mighty Name, Amen!

Affirmation:

I have the endurance I need to persevere and journey onward in my purpose no matter what happens along the way.

Reflective Question:

How can I be tenacious in my pursuit of purpose?

<u>Are You Ready?</u>

Are you living the life that God has called you to live? Are you living the life you were created and destined to live?

What does being ready or getting ready require? First and foremost, have a relationship with God. Without it, you can and will be led astray unto a path of destruction. Sometimes it's a destructive path of our own devices, and other times it's one that's been set up by the enemy. In either case, you need instructions, guidance, and protection as you are preparing for what's ahead.

"My sheep hear my voice, and I know them, and they follow me." *John 10:27 KJV*

"And a stranger will they not follow, but will flee from him: for they know not the voice of strangers." John 10:5 KJV

1. **Instructions** - The word of God gives us the greatest instructions and is literally the manuscript for our lives. When preparing for what God has for you to do, make sure to meditate on the word of God night and day.

    "This book of the law shall not depart out of thy mouth, but thou shalt meditate therein day and night, that thou mayest observe to do according to all that is written therein: for then thou shalt make

thy way prosperous, and then thou shalt have good
success." Joshua 1:8 KJV

2. **Guidance** The Holy Spirit provides guidance, not just
   to help us along the way, but in the readiness stage of
   our purpose. Holy Spirit speaks the heart and will of
   God to us so that we will not go outside of God's will
   for our lives. We must learn to take heed when the
   Holy Spirit speaks to us and leads us where God
   wants us to go.

   *"And do not bring sorrow to God's Holy Spirit by the
   way you live. Remember, he has identified you as his
   own, guaranteeing that you will be saved on the
   day of redemption." Ephesians 4:30 NLT*

3. **Protection** - We should never have any worries about
   what can cause us harm because God is our
   protector.

   *"No weapon that is formed against thee shall
   prosper; and every tongue [that] shall rise against
   thee in judgment thou shalt condemn. This [is] the
   heritage of the servants of the LORD, and their
   righteousness [is] of me, saith the LORD." Isaiah
   54:17 KJV*

   God is not just a protector of our physical beings, but
   he will protect us against the spiritual weapons that

are always against us. In the spirit realm is where our greatest battle is.

"For we wrestle not against flesh and blood, but against principalities, against powers, against the rulers of the darkness of this world, against spiritual wickedness in high [places]. 13 Wherefore take unto you the whole armour of God, that ye may be able to withstand in the evil day, and having done all, to stand." Ephesians 6:12-13 KJV

Prayer:
Father God, help me to take heed to your instructions, follow your guidance and lean into your protection as you ready me for my purpose. I trust you, Lord, and I love you. Thank you for keeping me out of the path of destruction.

Affirmation:
I have been given all I need by Abba Father to fully walk in my purpose.

Reflective Question:
How can I devote more time to studying the word of God, listening to the Holy Spirit and resting in the Lord?

Pursuit Of Purpose

Pursuit is simply defined as the act of following, the effort to secure or attain. Purpose is defined as the reason you were created.

What are you pursuing that is in direct opposition to your purpose? Have you ever given any thought to what your purpose may be? Or are you moving through life on your own agenda?

Have you ever watched crime or mystery shows? There is always the question of finding out who committed the crime and why. If you pay close attention, there is a strategy to getting to the bottom of "the why." Let's take a murder for instance.

It starts with asking questions, such as: "Who would have a motive to see this person dead? Who are the people in this person's life and who had direct contact with this person? Where did this person go hours or days leading up to their murder?"

Now think of these questions in terms of pursuing your purpose:

1. **What are your motives or reason for living?**
   Purpose gives you a reason to live. Besides the fact that you woke up this morning, there should be a clear indicator of why you wake up and do what you do. These indicators will help you to make choices that will further connect you to the right people and activities that will further you along your journey of purpose. This leads me to the next question.

2. **Who are the people in your life?**

   Not just who are your family members, but those people you confide in and share trusted information with. There is a saying, "Show me who your friends are and I will show you who you are." If the people you hold close to you are not bringing value to your life by providing sound advice, encouraging you beyond your comfort areas, and praying with and for you, then they could be part of the problem of why you are not in our purpose. Those that don't lift you up are bringing you down!

3. **What are you doing on a daily basis that brings value to your life?**

   Last but certainly not least, what are you doing for yourself that will bring you to your purpose and keep you there? Every second and every minute of the day counts. You must be a vigilant keeper of your time. Being mindful of how you spend your time will help you not waste it on thoughts or activities that are in direct opposition to your purpose.

Prayer: Father God, let my heart posture be one of a continuous desire to please you. Lord, reveal everything and everyone that will get in the way of me pursuing my purpose. In Jesus's Name, Amen!

Affirmation: I will chase after the things of God before I pursue anything else.

Reflective Question: What is taking my focus from pursuing my purpose?

We Must Remember God

God has chosen us. We are his people, we belong to the most high.

God decided in advance to adopt us into his own family by bringing us to himself through Jesus Christ. This is what he wanted to do, and it gave him great pleasure. Ephesians 1:5 NLT

God the creator of ALL chose us to represent his kingdom on earth. So let us not be puffed up in pride because we did not create ourselves, nor did we choose this life God has planned for us.

So in knowing this, why do we not consult God on how to operate in our purpose? Instead, we try to figure it out for ourselves and end up calling out to God anyway for help.

I want to encourage you to remember God first in all you do.
1. **Consult God first when making a decision - Proverbs 3:6 KJV** *In all thy ways acknowledge him, and he shall direct thy paths.*
2. **Seek God and his word daily - Matthew 6:33 KJV** *But seek ye first the kingdom of God, and his righteousness; and all these things shall be added unto you.*
3. **Pray fervently and without ceasing - James 5:16 NIV** *Therefore confess your sins to each other and pray for each other so that you may be healed. The prayer of a righteous person is powerful and effective.*
4. **Don't shrink back from who God has created you to be - Hebrews 10:39 NIV** *But we do not belong to those who*

shrink back and are destroyed, but to those who have faith and are saved.

5. **Acknowledge him all your ways - Proverbs 3:5-6 KJV** *Trust in the LORD with all thine heart, and lean not unto thine own understanding. In all thy ways acknowledge him, and he shall direct thy paths.*

6. **Die to self and your old ways of thinking - Colossians 3:2-3 NIV** *Set your minds on things above, not on earthly things. For you died, and your life is now hidden with Christ in God.*

7. **Put no one and nothing before God - *Exodus 20:3 KJV*** *"You shall have no other gods before me."*

Prayer:

Father God, Thank you for choosing me for such a time as this. Thank you for placing in me everything I need to be who you called me to be. Thank you for directing my path into purpose. I LOVE YOU LORD. In Jesus's Name, Amen!

Affirmation:

I have the mind of Christ and I can do ALL things through Christ that strengthens me.

Reflective Question: How can I make sure my life is fully aligned with the will of God?

Potential

having or showing the capacity to become or develop into something in the future

In Our Weakest Moments…

…Christ's strength is made perfect.

"And he said unto me, My grace is sufficient for thee: for my strength is made perfect in weakness. Most gladly, therefore, will I rather glory in my infirmities, that the power of Christ may rest upon me." 2 Corinthians 12:9 KJV

Weakness is a believer's superpower because you have the potential to allow God's strength to be made known in you if you are willing to submit to the almighty Father. Unfortunately, many of us have been taught, "Don't let them see your weakness." Weaknesses have been given a bad rep! Well, let's turn that around for your good.

Weakness is defined as the state or condition of lacking strength. Yet, this definition is contrary to what God says in his word. First of all, God says we lack no good thing in him. *"Even strong young lions sometimes go hungry, but those who trust in the LORD will lack no good thing." [Psalm 34:10 NLT]* So that means if we trust in the Lord, then we will not lack strength for God is our strength.

So again I ask you, why is it that you feel weakness is a bad thing? Let me guess, your weakness was taken advantage of and now you've vowed to never be weak again. Can I tell you a secret? That individual that made the foolish decision to take advantage of you was actually the weak one and they will have consequences to pay.

I do hope you forgive them so that unforgiveness does not allow bitterness into your heart.

Moving right along, remember this weakness, if given to God, has the amazing potential to be the greatest strength you've ever seen. God delights in using the foolish things of the world to confound the wise. *"But God hath chosen the foolish things of the world to confound the wise, and God hath chosen the weak things of the world to confound the things which are mighty…" 1 Corinthians 1:27 KJV*

Prayer:
Lord, use every area of weakness in my life to give you glory and honor. Help me to live in the shame of my weaknesses, but to trust you with them. Help me to heal from my past hurts that have caused me to have a hardened heart, and help me to forgive those who took advantage of me in my weakness. In Jesus's Name, Amen!

Affirmation:
God is made strong in my weakness!

Reflective Question: What areas in my life do I consider a weakness that really could be made into strength, if I only trust God?

All Circumstances Are Beneficial

All circumstances have the potential to power your purpose if put into proper perspective!

- **Circumstances that make you doubt** - When doubt creeps in, it's an opportunity for you to go deeper in your faith with the Lord. Doubt can lead to frustration and for many, they give up at this point or remain stagnant. As a believer, we are always invited to go even deeper with the Lord. Especially when your circumstances are causing you to doubt what the Lord has spoken over your life. It's a challenge that invites you to come back harder with what you know to be the truth of what God has promised you. It's similar to being bullied by someone "seemingly" bigger and stronger than you. You can choose to give in and get beat up every day, run away and hide, or come back with more confidence to stand up and face that bully head-on!

- **Circumstances that cause you to stumble** - are opportunities for you to get back up with greater resolve and a renewed sense of perspective. Stumbling gives us a chance to regroup and strategize differently because the vantage points are different when you have fallen. You now know what not to do and how to go forward in a different manner.

- **Circumstances that challenge your faith** - encourage us to get to God's word ourselves, not as a by-product of what others have to say about the Bible, but what you have taken the time to read, study and meditate on for yourself. I think all too often we become lazy in our faith and rely on the preaching, prophesying, and ministering of others to get us through, without us ever actually sitting down with the Bible for ourselves and receiving the revelations of God's word by way of the Holy Spirit. So when challenges arise that go against everything you have ever heard, see it as an opportunity to get into God's word for yourself. Be prepared to start experiencing the new and fresh revelation of what he has to say about your circumstances. Then you can confidently speak to that circumstance and it will obey because everything has to obey the word of God when spoken for the authority that Christ Jesus has given us. *So Jesus said to them, Because of your unbelief; for assuredly, I say to you, if you have faith as a mustard seed, you will say to this mountain, 'Move from here to there,' and it will move, and nothing will be impossible for you. Matthew 17:20 NKJV*

- **Circumstances that cause you to surrender-** will draw you nearer to God. Surrendering is not a bad thing especially when you surrender to God. It's like a wonderful trade-off of what you may have wanted versus what God actually has for you. I don't know about you, but getting what God has ordained to be mine from before the beginning of time sounds like a wonderful investment. *"Give, and it will be given to you: good measure, pressed down, shaken together, and running over will be put into your bosom. For with the same measure that you use, it will be measured back to you." Luke 6:38 NKJV*

Sounds like it has accrued some heavenly interest that will turn into an earthly overflow of abundance. Quite often we are reluctant to change course, give up on our way of doing things or just be still as God works quietly behind the scenes. I believe it's the unknowing, the uncertainty, and the feeling vulnerable that we do not like when it comes to surrendering. Unlike the world's way of surrendering, God's way of surrendering allows us to rest while he goes to work on our behalf. What great power that is to have the Almighty God-creator of ALL the universe working on our behalf. Almost sounds like an unfair advantage!

"Dear brothers and sisters, when troubles come your way, consider it an opportunity for great joy." James 1:2 NLT

Prayer:
Dear Father God, when trouble comes help me to seek your face before I seek your hand. Give me a spirit of praise that is released

from my lips, instead of grumbling and complaining. In Jesus's Name, Amen!

Affirmation:
I will rejoice when trouble knocks on my door, for I know that my faith is being challenged and will have an opportunity to increase.

Reflective Question:
What challenges have I faced that have pushed me further into my potential?

It's Not What You See

What you see happening in your life is not always as it seems, but how you perceive it. A renewed mind sees problems as potential. Have you ever worn glasses, whether sunglasses or reading glasses, and your lenses became dirty or fogged up? You had to take them off to clean them in order to see. Otherwise, your obscured view could have put you in harm's way. So, what if our vision is obscured by our past mistakes, our past hurts, and our past actions? Sometimes the past tries to go with us where it does not belong, into our future.

When something is being obscured it can be unclear and difficult to understand, even causing confusion and unnecessary complications within our lives. We can not allow our past to block our perception. How does one remove what's blocking their view? By cleaning your line of vision with a renewed mind. Think of your renewed mind like the cloth you would use to clean fogged-up-dirty glasses.

- A renewed mind replaces confusion with clarity
- A renewed mind provides simple solutions to complicated situations
- A renewed mind will see what's trying to stay hidden from your line of sight
- A renewed mind will know how to remove every obstacle in your way

Prayer:

Dear Father, I pray that my mind is renewed daily in Christ. I cast down every high imagination that exalts itself against the word God. I pray the visions and thoughts are not obscured by things of this world but are focused on the word of God. In Jesus' Name, Amen!

Affirmation:

I will keep my mind renewed in Christ Jesus daily!

Reflective Question:

What are some ways that I can keep my focus on Christ?

A Seed Of Greatness

God has planted a seed of Greatness within you. You have an assignment. No matter what obstacles or tests you face, he has chosen you. He has purposed and prepared you in your mother's womb. You have been endowed with a gift uniquely only to you, that Christ Jesus has placed within you. *"You made all the delicate, inner parts of my body and knit me together in my mother's womb." Psalm 139:13 NLT*

- Every seed that has been planted must grow!
- Every assignment that has been given must be completed!
- Every aspect of your life must produce fruit!
- Every test you face has an answer!
- Every call must be answered!

God is not a forceful God so he will not make you do anything. If you won't do what God has placed in you, then he will move on to the next. But why would you want to live your life incomplete? Living on unused, untapped, unrecognized potential. That's like eating uncooked or halfway-cooked meat. You will definitely get sick, and for what? Not only will you get sick, but you will still need to eat something else because you will still be hungry.

Don't live like this! Ask God to show you how to water the seeds of potential that have been planted within you so that you can complete the assignment(s) he has given you. And start producing the fruits of greatness!

Prayer:

Father God, I asked that you show me how to water the seeds of potential that you have planted within me. I desire to leave this world with all my assignments completed, living a life pleasing unto you. In Jesus's Name, Amen!

Affirmation:

I will not live an incomplete life.

Reflective Question:

What aspects of my life are not producing results?

Disadvantages Are Advantages

There is an advantage to every disadvantage. Learn to find the advantages in YOUR disadvantages. God loves doing the most from seemingly impossible situations; that's how he gets the greatest GLORY!

Having a disadvantage means an unfavorable circumstance or condition that reduces the chances of success or effectiveness. Perfect conditions for God to do his best work.

God's favor will give you the advantage in any and every situation. When every door is closed and there are no visible opportunities, God will make a way out of no way.

Some examples of disadvantages:
- Growing up in a broken home
- Past mistakes
- Bad decisions
- Living in an impoverished community
- Physical handicaps

All of these circumstances can make you feel downtrodden, with no hope. Yet even in the midst of these circumstances, God is still God. There is nothing too hard for God and nothing that can count you out from being chosen to do his greatest work.

Prayer:

Father God, open every door of opportunity that the enemy tried to close from me. I forgive myself for the bad decisions I made that put me on the path of destruction and distraction. I also forgive those in my past and in my life who, either knowingly or unknowingly, played a part in my unfavorable conditions. I pray the favor of the Lord is my portion and every wrong WILL BE made right. In Jesus's Name, Amen!

Affirmation:

I am at an advantage even when the world considers it a disadvantage because I place my trust in God.

Reflective Question:

What are some circumstances in my life that can be used by God to propel me forward to my potential?

More Than Enough

You have what you need to become who and what you are destined and dream to be with **faith**, **discipline**, **hard work**, and an open mind. With a new perspective, you can look at your life differently as you are being processed, pushed, purged, and prepared for greater.

- **FAITH** is believing in what you can not yet see. Giving us hope and confidence in what's to come.
  Hebrews 11:1 (KJV) "Now faith is the substance of things hoped for, the evidence of things not seen."
  Hebrews 11: (NLT) Faith is the confidence that what we hope for will actually happen; it gives us assurance about things we cannot see."

Faith will have you looking at your potential as the possibility to be something even greater. For instance, bakers look at flour as having the potential to be an assortment of baked goods: cookies, loaves of bread, pie crusts, etc. A chef looks at a piece of meat as having the potential to become a tasty meal that will feed his customers. A writer looks at the words on their paper as having the potential to become the next best-selling book. The common goal is to take what you have and build upon it. Your perspective to see your potential as being greater starts with having faith in the words God has spoken into your life, no matter how outlandish and strange they may be.

- **DISCIPLINE** or self-control is a fruit of the spirit, meaning as believers in Jesus Christ, we have been given a set of characteristics by the Holy Spirit within that sets us apart from those who do not believe.

But the Holy Spirit produces this kind of fruit in our lives: love, joy, peace, patience, kindness, goodness, faithfulness, gentleness, and self-control. There is no law against these things! Galatians 5:22-23 NLT

Discipline will help you to get through the process of fortifying your potential into something much more substantial. Discipline will allow you to focus on the outcome, rather than how much the process hurts and is making you uncomfortable. Discipline shifts your perspective from that of pain to one of purpose. Being self-controlled is not about being rigid and unmovable. It is quite the opposite! Self-control in the Lord will have you move, go, and do what the Lord has instructed you to do, even at the cost of losing everything YOU love. All because it is what the Lord wants and we obey because we love him and seek to please him by doing his will. *"But those who obey God's word truly show how completely they love him. That is how we know we are living in him." 1 John 2:5 NLT*

- **HARD WORK** is a by-product of wanting to get "it" done. What that "it" may be is really up to you. Since we are discussing potential, then let's dive into what happens when you apply intentional hard work to potential.

Sometimes people work hard all their lives and have nothing to really show for it. They have stayed on a job and given it their all, only to make ends meet but never really living to their fullest potential. Some people work really hard to become someone they will be proud of but are never really happy with themselves or love themselves when it is all said and done.

Hard work that's intentional and led by the spirit of the living God produces a harvest that is recognized by its fruits. There should be evident signs in your life that you are working hard to your potential. You will notice a purging of old habits, negative mindsets, and lackluster individuals just to name a few. Hard work will also push you past your comfort zone. Outside your comfort zone is where your potential really has the opportunity to grow.

Having an open mind or rather an open mind to the things of the Lord will not only shift your perspective on how you see your potential, but it will also increase your faith, power up your level of discipline, and shift the momentum of your hard work!

Prayer:
Lord, you said in your word that it is by faith that we please you, and so I come to you in need of more faith to believe what you have said about me. Lord, I also need help in having an open mind to shift my perspective. I want to believe what you see in me so that I can be more disciplined and intentional in how I spend my time and what I exert my efforts into. In Jesus's Name, Amen!

Affirmation:

I am who I need to become. I just need to have the faith, discipline, and hard work to see my potential through.

Reflective Question:

How can I incorporate more faith into my life, and in what areas do I need to be more disciplined and work harder?

No Matter What!

No matter where you're from or what mistakes you've made, you must believe that you still have the potential to be GREAT. It says so right in *1 John 4:4: "You, dear children, (1) are from God and have overcome them, (2) because the one who is in you (3) is greater than the one who is in the world."*

Do you believe that mistakes have the potential to be purposeful? Let's first look at the definition of mistakes: *an action or judgment that is misguided or wrong - inaccuracy, slip, or miscalculation.*

When we make a mistake, it is usually on our way to doing something on purpose, but along the way, we may have miscalculated or were inaccurate in our judgment. No one ever intentionally decides to be wrong in their decision-making or actions. We usually have an end goal in mind, a reason or purpose for what we are setting out to do.

When does a mistake turn into malicious intent in wrongdoing? This happens when instead of acknowledging your mistakes and redirecting your path, you decide to move forward in the error of your ways. Here is where there is an opportunity for potential purpose:

1) Acknowledge your mistakes
2) Accept you were wrong
3) Ask for forgiveness
4) Seek out the Lord's help
5) Move forward in the Lord's will

Prayer:

Father God, I seek your will for my life. I acknowledge and confess the error of my ways and repent for my sins. I want what you want for me and so I desire a clean heart. Clean up the areas of my life, mind, and spirit that are not like you. In Jesus' Name, Amen!

Affirmation:

I WILL TRUST THE LORD!

Reflective Question:

What mistakes have I made that I have yet to forgive myself for?

Faith Is Potential Activated

Faith is your superpower and when you apply it to any situation, it will turn things around in your favor. But first, we have to believe in order to please God and see the promises of God manifest in our lives. *"And it is impossible to please God without faith." Anyone who wants to come to him must believe that God exists and that he rewards those who sincerely seek him. [Hebrews 11:6 NLT]* The entire chapter of Hebrews 11 talks about how various individuals in the Bible moved in faith in God's word and promises alone!

- *Faith turns disasters into open doors:* Imagine losing your home, your family, your job, losing everything you loved and knew. Now imagine God giving you back everything you lost even greater. (Read Job's story in the Bible) He is the greatest example of losing everything yet he did not give up on God.

- *Faith turns frustrations into motivations:* Have you ever been so frustrated with waiting on someone else to get something done for you that you end up just doing it yourself? You could be frustrated with a specific set of circumstances in your life and you make a decision to do something about it so that the outcome is more in your favor. Perhaps you are just fed up with the job you are on and decide to update your resume and look elsewhere for employment opportunities. These are just a few examples of using your frustrations as a source of motivation to shift circumstances and outcomes.

- **_Faith turns obstacles into opportunities:_** An obstacle is anything (object, perspective, thought process, person, etc) that is blocking or preventing you from making progress or moving forward. Yet, there is a lesson, blessing, and opportunity in everything, only if we are willing to see the potential that lies before us. In order to turn an obstacle into an opportunity, you have to believe it to be possible, even without ever seeing it done before. That's really faith in action! Once you are willing to believe, then you take action by shifting the obstacles into an opportunistic position. For example, If there was a chair blocking you from entering a room, would you not enter that room, or would you move the chair out of the way? I am pretty sure you would move the chair to the side and enter the room. An even greater opportunity is using that exact chair to be seated in that room.

- **_Faith turns adversities into avenues:_** Hardships, trials, and tribulations can really have an adverse effect on our faith if we choose to let it! Faith has been given to us to use in EVERY situation! Each hardship we face is an avenue to increase our faith and grow a deeper relationship with God. The trials we experience are a test of our faith and an avenue to grow stronger in our knowledge of who God is in our lives. The tribulations that come will cause some suffering, but in that suffering is an avenue of a deeper trust for God because you know only he can comfort you the best.

Faith, genuine faith, and faith in God are essential to the believers.

"But without faith [it is] impossible to please [him]: for he that cometh to God must believe that he is, and [that] he is a rewarder of them that diligently seek him." Hebrews 11:6 KJV

When your faith increases, you will begin to understand that you possess something on the inside that keeps you standing when life experiences toss you from side to side. You must raise your faith level up a few notches to match the word of God. The increase in faith is a by-product of trusting God. Trusting God comes from experiencing him. For some of us, it is not easy to trust God because we compare him to humans in our life that have failed us too many times for us to count. God is not like us; he does not make promises he will not keep, he does not lie, and he does not change his mind. Once he speaks a thing it shall be done!

"God is not a man, so he does not lie. He is not human, so he does not change his mind. Has he ever spoken and failed to act? Has he ever promised and not carried it through?" Numbers 23:19 NLT

God has placed in us many amazing gifts, qualities, and characteristics that are just potential waiting to be used. If we use up everything inside of us then we end up dying with regrets. Yet, how can we begin to tap in and start using the tools God placed in us from the beginning to help us in life when times become tumultuous? You must start with faith! Believe it is there.

When you were a toddler and you first began to walk, you trusted your legs to take you places. Your legs have always been on your body and with you, but it wasn't until your parents encouraged you to use them that you began to stand and take steps. Well, God is that parent that is encouraging you to use your stored potential by allowing those unpleasant life experiences to surface so that you may start moving in faith. As you take your first steps in trusting God and the "legs" he equipped you with, the solutions to your problems will present themselves. You will find that you will no longer be tossed about with worry, but you will be standing strong in faith.

Prayer:
Dearest Father God, I want to experience a new level in you. I want to go deeper and develop a more profound relationship with you. God I thank you for equipping me with all I need to be great. Lord help me to not compare my life or myself to others, but stay focused on you! In Jesus' Name, Amen!

Affirmation:
Greater is **HE** that is in me, than they that are in the world!

Reflective Question:
In what ways can I increase my faith in Christ Jesus?

It's Time!

Your qualities and abilities are developed in the seasons of trial and tribulations. It is time you start recognizing your potential! Stop counting yourself out!

Recognizing your potential can be unfamiliar territory especially if you have spent most of your life doubting yourself and being caught up in the opinions and approval of others. You see, God made you well-equipped to do everything He has chosen you for. **God chose you!** So, why would he not provide you with what you need?

Here are some scriptures to meditate on that will give you assurance in your potential (Write them out on a post-it notes and place them where they can be easily seen):

    A. *[2 Timothy 3:17 NIV] so that the servant of God may be thoroughly equipped for every good work.*

    B. *[Hebrews 13:21 NIV] equip you with everything good for doing his will, and may he work in us what is pleasing to him, through Jesus Christ, to whom be glory forever and ever. Amen.*

    C. *[1 Corinthians 1:26-29 NLT] Remember, dear brothers and sisters, that few of you were wise in the world's eyes or powerful or wealthy when God called you. Instead, God chose things the world considers foolish in order to shame those who think they are wise. And he chose things that are powerless to shame those who are powerful. God chose things despised by the world, things counted as nothing at all, and used them to bring to nothing what the world considers important. As a result, no one can ever boast in the presence of God.*

Prayer:

Thank you, Father God, for choosing to use me to bring you glory. I am your servant, who you have thoroughly equipped to do your will and work on this earth. I will not allow what I experience throughout life to make me feel less than who God has called me to be. Even my trials and tribulations have a much greater purpose than to cause strife; they are to build character and to draw out every bit of my potential and I count it all joy. In Jesus's Mighty Name, Amen!

Affirmation:

I thank God for my season of trials and tribulations, for they have uncovered the true potential within myself.

Reflective Question:

Which of my qualities and abilities are being built up in this current season of my life and how can I surrender to the refiner's process?

Developed For Your Future

Tap in and find your potential:

- **Usefulness -** Every part of your story and your life from the time of conception is useful in the kingdom of God. There is nothing wasted or too bad for God not to use for HIS GLORY! -[Romans 8:28 KJV]

- **Dedication -** When you give your life to Christ, you are dedicated to being used by God. Your life is no longer your own, you become an important vessel of change that will impact the nations. -[1 Corinthians 6:19-20]

- **Commitment -** Commitment to God starts in your heart then your actions follow.- [Proverbs 23:7]

- **Eagerness -** When you are eager to do the things of God by putting him first, then you will start to see those things you hoped and prayed for come to pass. - [Matthew 6:33]

- **Responsibility -** It is our responsibility to be good stewards over what God has given freely (time, gifts, free will) - [1 Peter 4:10]

- **Versatility** - Being adaptable to change is important when listening and obeying God. We may have our own plans, but God's perfect will should always come first. - [Matthew 6:10]

- **Creativity** - We are creativity personified, God has chosen us as his most precious masterpiece to be put on display for the world to see. So let your light shine, and begin tapping into who God created you to be. - [Ephesians 2:10]

- **Adaptability** - It doesn't matter what you have done in the past or what has happened to you, God can and will still use you. [2 Corinthians 5:17]

The development of our truest selves starts before the time of our conception. You see God has already chosen, designated, and designed a life for us that would be conducive to our growth potential. We may have been sidetracked, distracted, and discouraged due to mishaps that have happened along the way of this journey called life. Yet, if we return to our Father's bosom, open the word of God, and rededicate our lives unto him, we will find that all is not lost.

Prayer:
Father God, I am ready to tap into you ALL you created me to be. I will no longer waste time doubting myself or you. Thank you, Holy Spirit, for your guidance on this journey to become the everything I

was chosen to be. I will leave no potential on the table, but instead, seek Godly wisdom and understanding on how to operate in the potential given to me. In Jesus' Mighty Name, Amen!

Affirmation:
I accept that God had already chosen me before my conception.

Reflective Question:
What area of my potential will I develop first and why?

Power

a right or authority that is given or delegated to a person or body

The 7 powers of the Holy Spirit: wisdom, understanding, counsel, fortitude, knowledge, piety, and fear of the Lord

Power In Contentment

"Not that I was ever in need, for I have learned how to be content with whatever I have." Philippians 4:11 NLT

Paul learned the secret of being content, no matter what situation or experience he faced. He understood the power of being at peace. Not complacent, not stagnated, not procrastinating, but content in the manner of understanding how to draw on the power of Jesus Christ.

Being content allows you to rest in the knowledge of knowing that God has your back no matter the circumstance. The power in that is being able to be unmoved by what's going on around you. Contentment is a peaceful state of existence that is not contingent on any one set of happenings. When you are content, you value being still and trusting God. As a matter of fact, you are able to hold your own even when it seems like there is no progress where you are because you understand that God is always working on your behalf.

Being content is not to be confused with being complacent. When you are content you are completely trusting God to provide, supply, and be your resource. Yet, you are not just waiting around doing nothing. You are still very much on assignment. The power of being content is knowing when to move and when to go in accordance with God's will for your life.

- Learn to be content in your season of singleness so that you don't settle or rush into a soul tie.
- Learn to be content in your season of building so that you can understand what the Lord has for you ahead.
- Learn to be content in your season of rest, so that you may be prepared for the journey ahead.
- Learn to be content as a student of God's word so that you can be also a doer of his word.
- Learn to be content in your season of walking alone so that you don't rely on the approval of man, but seek God's face first each and every time.
- Learn to be content in a season of silence so that you may know the Father's voice when he speaks!

Prayer:
Dearest Father God, Help me to be content in every season I am in my life. I pray that in my time of resting in your presence, I will learn to be silent so that I may hear you clearly. I pray that I do not become complacent in my season of contentment. In Jesus' Name, Amen!

Affirmation:
I will operate in my power of being content wherever God leads.

Reflective Question:
Am I content in every area of my life?

Power Starts Within The Mind

There is power in a renewed mind. When our minds are renewed, we have a different outlook on life, and we perceive our struggles and challenges differently. Our lifestyle changes, our thought patterns are different, and our attitude changes. - *"And be not conformed to this world: but be ye transformed by the renewing of your mind, that ye may prove what [is] that good, and acceptable, and perfect, will of God." Romans 12:2 KJV*

Recognizing the power of your mind is the first step to walking in power.
- Your thoughts lead to actions, whether you realize it or not.
- Start paying attention to your daily thoughts.
- Make notes of some fleeting thoughts you have.

What are some of the first thoughts about yourself when trouble arises? What are you telling yourself about the circumstances you encounter (whether good or bad)?

You may be wondering, "Okay, so my thinking is not where it should be. How do I "renew" my mind and change that?" Well, let's take a look at the word *renew*. It means to give a new appearance, to refresh, restore, rebuild, or repair. So, in order to renew your mind, you have to align your thoughts with those of Christ and that starts with reading His Word. How can one expect to renew their mind from its old ways if they do not have the proper thought patterns to replace it with? Start by looking up scriptures that talk about who God says you are to Him. For instance, when you feel a lack of confidence and feel defeated by the circumstances before you, tell yourself this: *"I will praise You, for I am fearfully [and] wonderfully made; Marvelous are Your works, And [that] my soul knows very well." [Psalm 139:14 NKJV]*

This will shift your perspective from how difficult your circumstances are to how wonderfully marvelous God has created you, and so there is nothing you can not do.

Prayer:
Father God, not only do I want to renew my mind, I want a renewed life that is refreshed, restored, rebuilt, or repaired in you. In Jesus' Name, Amen!

Affirmation:
I align my thoughts with Christ Jesus.

Reflective Question:
What thought patterns do I need to replace in order to renew my mind?

Faith Is Not An Option

Faith is not an option, but a MUST!

As Christians, we can not survive without exercising the Power of our faith.

"Just as the body is dead without breath, so also faith is dead without good works." James 2:26 NLT

As Christians, we cannot thrive without actively engaging the power of our faith.

"Just as the body is dead without breath, so also faith is dead without good works." James 2:26 NLT

Good works reflect a deliberate effort towards a desired outcome. For example, you might exercise with the goal of losing weight. Similarly, faith involves setting your sights on a goal, desire, need, or want, trusting that God will collaborate with you to achieve it. Putting faith into action means mapping out the end result from the start and taking concrete steps towards realizing it.

Prayer:
Lord Almighty, Grant me the strength to actively engage the power of my faith. As I strive toward the goals and desires of my heart,

may I always remember that faith without works is lifeless, much like a body without breath. Help me to embody the teachings of James, showing my faith through my actions and efforts. May my intentions be clear and my plans well-laid, with the trust that You are my partner in every endeavor. Guide me to put my faith into action, not just in hopes and prayers, but also in the steps I take to manifest Your blessings. Let each deed I perform be a testament to my faith, bringing me closer to the outcomes You have ordained. In Your holy name, I pray. Amen.

Affirmation:
I am empowered to manifest my faith through actions, knowing that each step I take is guided by God. With clarity of intention and purposeful efforts, I align my goals with divine guidance, trusting that God partners with me in achieving my heart's desires.

Reflective Question:
What specific actions can I take today to demonstrate my faith and align my efforts with God's guidance toward achieving my goals?

When I Am Weak...

I can say, **"Let the weak say they are strong." Isaiah 40:29 NLT** —
He gives power to the weak and strength to the powerless.

Your power doesn't stem from how strong you appear to others.
Instead, it comes from letting God's Spirit strengthen you in your
moments of vulnerability. For example, many view tears as a sign
of weakness, yet there's a profound strength in allowing oneself to
be vulnerable in front of others. Vulnerability is not a weakness! It
is a brave act to confront and share your true emotions. This
honesty fosters healing, growth, and real connections, showing
that true strength often lies in the willingness to be authentic.
Embrace these moments of openness for they are the gateway to
deeper understanding and spiritual resilience. Remember, each
time you choose transparency over concealment, you not only
liberate yourself but also empower others to embrace their truths.

Prayer:
Heavenly Father, in moments of weakness and doubt, when my
own strength falters and I feel overwhelmed, I come before You
seeking solace and guidance. Remind me, Lord, that true power
does not stem from my outward might or the facade of resilience,
but from Your Spirit dwelling within me. In my weakest hours, let
Your grace be my fortitude, Your love my courage, and Your
wisdom my guide. May I surrender to You, allowing Your Spirit to
shine, transforming trials into testimony and weakness into
worship. Strengthen me with Your heavenly might so that in every
breath and step, Your glory is revealed. Amen.

Affirmation:

I am strengthened not by my might, but by the Spirit of God within me. In my vulnerabilities, His power is made perfect, transforming my challenges into channels of divine strength and grace.

Reflective Question:

How can I better recognize and embrace my moments of weakness as opportunities for God's strength to manifest in my life?

The Processes Of Life

As you deal with the process of life, you understand that it is to manifest the power of God through you. Life is not about you, it's about others. So in every situation, we should give God the glory and praise.

Everything has a process it must go through and in that process, the completion of what's to come is made evident.

Imagine what a loaf of bread goes through before it reaches your local grocery store or even your kitchen. The ingredients that are needed to make the bread must be combined together: sifted, shaken, stirred, whisked, and mixed into one. Then comes the fire as the bread is placed in the oven to be baked. After the oven comes the cooling, then the slicing (if it's sliced bread) or straight to packaging, shipped to the store, and finally in your home to be eaten. If done right, the bread will be delicious, fulfilling, and worth what you paid for it.

Now, let's break this down when it comes to the process of life for us humans.

1. God instills certain qualities, characteristics, gifts, talents, and personalities in us that work together to create who we are his child. This is the mixing of the ingredients.
2. Certain trials and tribulations help to process us in various areas of our lives. This is considered the fire that brings out the best in us.

3. The cooling process is when you get a chance to see the glory of God's hand on your life once the smoke clears. Then you begin to make sense of it all and see how everything you've been through was not in vain.
4. Here lies the power of it all. You take every aspect of your process, the good, the bad, and the ugly, and start to embrace it all. Using the lessons and testimonials as a way to help others.

Prayer:
Thank you, Father God, for manifesting your miracle working power in my life, through trials and tribulation. I know that I will suffer as Christ did and I count it all joy. In Jesus' Name, Amen!

Affirmation:
I embrace every aspect of my life's journey because it is all important.

Reflective Question:
How can I use what I went through as a testimony to help others?

God Has Given Us Power

Within us, there is power by way of the Holy Spirit, given to by God, but we have to choose to use it. ***"For I can do everything through Christ, who gives me strength." Philippians 4:13 NLT***

Imagine being given a secret weapon that only you know about, know how to use, and know when to use it. Imagine also facing imminent danger and never using your secret weapon to protect or help yourself. Instead, you lay there and die. This is what it is like when we come face to face with certain situations in our lives that we have been given the power to overcome, yet we "choose" to worry, complain, or even worse, do nothing about it because fear paralyzed us. Believe it or not, worrying, complaining, and being fearful are ALL choices.

In Philippians 4:13, Paul talks about being able to do **EVERYTHING** through Christ who strengthens him. The keyword here is **everything**! Let's take a deeper look at the word everything: it means all things, every single thing.
1) We must first know we can know to do all things with Christ.
2) We must then understand there is nothing we can't do with Christ.
3) We must accept Christ's strength as our own so that we can go forth and do all things.

These are not just simple words of encouragement, but facts and instructions to live by as we carry out God's plan for our lives.

Prayer:
Dearest Father God, I can do all things through Christ that strengthens me and I live in the power of the Lord as I carry out God's plans for my life. In Jesus' Name, Amen!

Affirmation:
I accept Christ's strength as my own.

Reflective Question:
Have I allowed certain circumstances to hinder me from overcoming challenges in life?

You Have The Power To Change

Realize you have the power to change your life..

Change Your Life by **Serving God:**
To serve is such an honor, in any capacity, because you are setting aside your own needs, desires, and wants for those of another. Serving is a selfless act that requires a genuine heart and genuine intentions. When you are serving, you do not and should not expect recognition. The definition of serving is to perform duties or services for another. In **Matthew 6:33**, it says, **"Seek the Kingdom of God above all else, and live righteously, and he will give you everything you need." (NLT)** When we seek to serve God in every area of our lives, we do not have to worry about what we will eat, drink, or where we will lay our heads. God literally will take care of our every need! Knowing your every need is met, is a life-changing revelation, the freedom and peace of mind that comes with knowing the creator of the world has your back 1000%.

Change Your Circumstances by **Obeying God:**
Obedience to God is not begrudgingly saying, "Yes, Lord," and then complaining the entire time while doing what the Lord has asked of you. It's cheerfully and graciously being obedient to God's instructions because you understand God knows what's best for you. There are also blessings in being obedient to God's word. In **Deuteronomy 28:1-13**, the blessings listed are as follows: God will increase your territory, everything you touch, everywhere you go,

and whatever you do will be blessed. You will have generational wealth, influence, and **POWER**!

Change Your Viewpoint by **Loving God:**
Loving God should not be contingent on us having our prayer requests answered. We should love God because he is a good-good father and he first loved us. ***"We love him, because he first loved us." [1 John 4:19 KJV]*** We understand God's love for us from a child's point of view, and then we understand that God would never do anything to hurt us, even when our circumstances and pain try to tell us differently. As a loving parent, God never intended for our lives to cause us pain; therefore, when he saw that our sins were consuming us, he sent his Son to free us from the death of our sins. ***"This is love: not that we loved God, but that he loved us and sent his Son as an atoning sacrifice for our sins." [1 John 4:10 NIV]***

And so there is power in knowing that NOTHING can separate us from God's love for us. ***"...neither height nor depth nor anything else in all creation, will be able to separate us from the love of God that is in Christ Jesus our Lord." [Romans 8:39 NIV]***

Change Your Mind by **Hearing God:**
God is always speaking, we must choose to listen. Yet in order to know God's voice you must first recognize his voice by the words he speaks. His words are there for us to meditate on, we just have to choose to get to know God by studying his word daily for ourselves. ***"So then faith [cometh] by hearing, and hearing by the word of God." [Romans 10:17 KJV]*** When you understand God's

word, you are able to renew your mind when thoughts that don't align with what God has said come.

Prayer:
Dearest Father God, I love you and live to serve you. Amen!

Affirmation:
The change that is happening in my life has given me the power to be who God has designed me to be.

Reflective Question:
What changes are happening currently that I am finding difficult to adjust to?

Nothing Shall Hurt You

"Behold, I give unto you power to tread on serpents and scorpions, and over all the power of the enemy: and nothing shall by any means hurt you." Luke 10:19 KJV

When God says in his word that **nothing shall** hurt you, he meant it. Yet we go through life experiencing pain and suffering at the hands of others and ourselves. And so you may be wondering why this is. Well let's first examine the meaning of these two words:

- Shall: expressing the future tense
- Nothing: not anything; no single thing

God, being omnipresent, is very much aware of what the future holds for you and can foresee the things that will try to cause you harm. So, him being the amazing father that he is, has provided you with ways and tools to get out of harm's way.

If you are reading this, then that means you are alive. So why are you choosing to let what tried to kill you, but didn't, keep you bound in spiritual death.

The only way you succumb to the things that "tried" to take you out, is if you have chosen to give up and THERE IS NO POWER in giving up!

A lot of situations and circumstances can be avoided if we only use what God has given us, which is the Holy Spirit, his word, prayers, our relationship with God and our ears to hear him speak. God is always speaking and will let us know when and how to move to avoid impending dangers. We must choose to listen and obey, but often our ignorance of the word and lack of knowledge of who God really is cause us to misunderstand the power we hold as joint heirs to the kingdom of God. As a parent or a responsible adult, you wouldn't let a child go outside and play without being properly dressed for the weather. You would also give that child instructions and warnings on what to do and not to do, where to go and where not to go, who they can play with and who to stay away from. This is the same of God, he will not send us out into the world without properly preparing us with warnings and instructions.

Will you claim your power by stepping into the deep with God to learn of who he is so that you can rise up in who you are?

Prayer:
Dearest God, I am grateful for your protection and provision. I will step into the deep with you so that I may further see where you want to take me. In Jesus Name, Amen!

Affirmation:
I will not allow anything or anyone to prevent me from going deeper with the Lord.

Reflective Question:
How have I gotten in my own way of seeing God move through me?

Thank You, Father

We thank God for giving us strength, power, and wisdom.

" For God has not given us a spirit of fear and timidity, but of power, love, and self-discipline."2 Timothy 1:7 NLT

Thankfulness is a most powerful weapon that can confuse the enemies of our soul. Have you ever had a moment where you were feeling doubtful and then you started remembering all the moments God showed up in your life? Your attitude immediately changed because your perspective shifted. Thankfulness will literally shift the atmosphere and confuse the enemy. Imagine being in the middle of a war and you break out in song and dance. Yeah, sounds crazy, huh? But then in 2 Chronicles 20, the Lord instructs Jehoshaphat to do just that when they were set to face the armies of the Moabites, Ammonites, and some of the Meunites in war. These opposing armies were so confused that they ended up fighting and killing each other and not even touching Jehoshaphat's people.

Another form of thankfulness is praise! The definition of praise is the expression of respect and gratitude as an act of worship. That expression can be in the form of song, dance, art, prayers, or the uplifting of your hands while pouring out your heart to God in your devotional time. When you are in a posture of praise and thankfulness, you are positioning yourself for the power of Almighty God to work through you.

Prayer:

Father God, I give ALL the praise and honor. You are the head of my life Lord and the only source of my power. My life will give you glory. In Jesus Name, Amen!

Affirmation:

Thankfulness is my position of power.

Reflective Question:

How can I be more thankful on a regular basis?

Understanding The Race

Well beloved, when you understand the race was not given to the swift, nor the strong but to the one who endured to the end, you can then realize you have a purpose, you possess potential, and you have power. You must realize the importance of utilizing the faith God has given you as his chosen one.

Understanding means that you have sought out your heavenly father to gain access to the wisdom to operate in your power. Because what is a power tool if you don't know how to use it? It becomes useless and quite possibly dangerous in the wrong hands.

Prayer:
Father God, help me to see and understand what I am chosen for and how to go about walking in the power and authority of Christ Jesus. In Jesus' Name, Amen!

Affirmation:
I will not lean unto my own understanding, but seek God's wise counsel every step of the way as I walk in my power.

Reflective Question:
Am I walking in power with the understanding of who I am and who God has chosen me to be?

Conclusion

As you journey through life's highs and lows, enduring its trials and triumphs, keep this book close at hand. It is meant to be a constant reminder of your identity and divine purpose. Remember, you are not just wandering through life; you are deliberately chosen for a purpose that transcends what the eye can see.

Consider the powerful message of *John 15:16: "You did not choose me, but I chose you and appointed you so that you might go and bear fruit—fruit that will last—and so that whatever you ask in my name the Father will give you."* This verse reassures you that God's selection is intentional and empowering. Despite the obstacles, you are destined to flourish. The secret is to stay committed, connected, and consistent in every aspect of life. Embrace your God-ordained destiny, a future filled with hope and purpose.

Let this book be a frequent reference that reignites your belief in your immense potential. It is a testament that you have the ability to achieve your dreams and aspirations, overcoming any barriers with determination and faith.

Furthermore, remember the power bestowed upon you, as *2 Timothy 1:7* reminds us: *"For God hath not given us the spirit of fear; but of power, and of love, and of a sound mind."* In times of uncertainty or challenge, these words should be your refuge.

Embrace your identity in Christ, and steadfastly follow your chosen path. Engage in prayer, immerse yourself in God's word, reflect on it, apply its teachings, and trust in the unfolding journey. This book is more than a guide; it's a beacon, illuminating your path with the strength and courage you possess through God's enduring love and wisdom.

About the Author...

Minister Diretha Jennings

Minister Diretha Jennings, born and raised in Chicago, Illinois is a proud member of the St. John Baptist Temple of Chicago, IL., under the leadership of Pastor Benjamin E. Davis. She is a humble, anointed, compassionate, funny, and loving woman of God who believes in giving God her all.

As a motivational speaker and mentor, Minister Diretha J., has been afforded the opportunity to speak and teach at various conferences, events, women's day services, and churches throughout the United States.

She is the creator and organizer of Chosen For A Purpose, Inc. where the goal is to find creative ways to serve, witness, empower, enlighten, encourage and equip the people of God.

Minister Diretha J. lives by Philippians 4:13: " I can do all things through Christ which strengthen me."

Contact the Author:
Email: chosenforapurpose@gmail.com
Facebook: Chosen For A Purpose
Instagram: @chosenforapurpose

www.ingramcontent.com/pod-product-compliance
Lightning Source LLC
Chambersburg PA
CBHW051701090426
42736CB00013B/2490